MW01199355

SUCCESS AND FAILURE

BASED ON

REASON AND REALITY

BY

HAMIS KIGGUNDU

ISBN: 978-1719-8695-4-6

Distributed By Ham Enterprises (U) Limited,

Located at:

Ham Towers

P.O.Box 2183

Makerere Hill Road

Kampala, Uganda

Email: hamenterprises2009@gmail.com

I DEDICATE THIS BOOK

TO MY PARENTS

MR AND MRS HARUNA
SEGAWA

AND

TO MY COUNTRY – UGANDA

"For God and my country"

TABLE OF CONTENTS

1

INTRODUCTION

I was born on 10th-Febuary, 1984. I am a Ugandan by birth, born and raised in Uganda. A son of Mr. and Mrs. Haruna Segawa. I had my primary, secondary and university education in Uganda. I hold a Bachelor's degree in Law from the School of Law at Makerere University, Kampala, Uganda.

I can proudly say I am a successful prominent businessman mainly trading in real estate. I own a chain of commercial properties in my country and in other parts of the world. I mainly trade as HAM ENTERPRISES (U) LTD in Uganda, trade as HAM INTERNATIONAL UK LTD in the United Kingdom, trade as HAM INTERNATIONAL LTD in the United

States of America and equally trade as SKYLIGHT INVESTMENTS in South Africa. I am currently employing more than 1,200 people.

Success is generally a gradual process just like life and growing up. When a child is born they start by crawling, then they walk and then finally run. If you try to run before walking you will fall. I took gradual steps to get to where I am today and still on my path to where I want to be.

In the first years of my university studies, my parents gave me some small reasonable capital to start business. I started small and locally, trading in the buying of commodities and merchandise from first hand importers from abroad and selling them at a profit. At that stage, I had so many ups and downs but still managed to grow my capital and progressed to a firsthand importer and started importing commodities from countries like China, Thailand, Hong Kong and Dubai and selling them in wholesale not just to Ugandans but also to customers from neighboring countries like Kenya, Tanzania, Burundi,

Congo and Sudan.

From wholesale business, I grew my capital so fast that I upgraded to real estate, mainly buying and selling land and properties at a profit. I finally progressed to constructing and owning my own commercial properties. That is how I have come to own a number of properties at the moment. Currently, I am into large scale industrialization, mainly focusing on the area of agro processing and value addition.

Uganda has very good fertile soil, very good favorable climate and a large young energetic population yet mainly dependent on imports with limited exports. I want to create demand for farmers' produce by putting up integrated agro processing industries which will encourage most Ugandans to move into agriculture since the land is fertile and the climate is conducive. By creating demand for farmers' produce, I will have provided a source of income for a reasonable number of Ugandans.

I choose agro processing now because all I have done so far is limited to my individual success. I want to do something that will not only grow my economic empire but equally create a positive reasonable change to my country. From my personal experience, I have come to learn that individual success does not count when living in a poor society. My desire now is to do something that not only widens my economic empire but also benefits my country.

When we travel abroad, as we go through the airport terminals, we are never judged by who we are or how much money we have on our bank accounts but judged by the passports we hold and our country of origin. Being successful in a poor society is partial success, that's why I am currently investing in agro processing and value addition to not only grow my empire but also make a difference in my society.

With agro processing, we are focusing on promoting import substitution. With this, I intend to mainly produce most of the commodities that we import from foreign countries. This will reduce the amount of money that leaves the country as expense which would have facilitated growth not limited to me by to my country as well.

Agro processing and value addition doesn't only target the domestic market but also the regional and the international market. It will, therefore, increase our national income, and in the long run, our monetary currency value will stabilise and ultimately this will lead to stable progress and development as a nation.

With agro processing and value addition, we can create hundreds of thousands of jobs for Ugandans both directly and indirectly; directly as company employees in different sectors like in demonstration farms, in sales and marketing, and indirectly by buying their farm produce hence giving them income.

Agro processing and value addition if successfully achieved, it will increase the country's tax base. Currently Uganda has a population of 42 million people but approximately only 1 million are tax payers meaning close to 41 million people are depending on only 1 million taxpayers.

By creating demand for farm produce, if only half of the 41 million till their land for food and cash crops, we would have created income for them. Government would then tax that income thereby widening the tax base; government will, therefore, be able to get more revenue to provide secondary services like roads, water and electricity to the citizens. That is the kind of positive change I'm looking forward to in our society.

It is important to note that it all has to be a gradual process because it requires a lot of capital and long term investment. It may sound so complicated but it is possible. Even the longest journey begins with the first step. I have taken the first steps; maybe when other businessmen see and appreciate my efforts, they will follow and together, we can collectively make this big dream come true. I have invested a lot of money in research on agro processing and value addition.

It is so huge an investment that I personally do not only see it as just the future of my company's success but equally as the only reasonable, realistic, straight and quick path to the development of our country and the best solution to Uganda's current economic problems. Big ideas that shape entire generations always start somewhere. I plan to risk all I have got on agro processing and value addition.

The permanent solution to Uganda's economic problem should come from us and sustainable development should come from the roots. It is every Ugandan's natural obligation to see Uganda develop not by simply talking about it like most Ugandans do but by putting in collective effort towards the national budget through especially paying taxes. An effective agro processing and value addition system will increase our individual and national income through import substitution from the domestic market and promotion of exports from the regional and international markets.

We can widen the tax base from the current 1 million tax payers to at least 21 million tax payers, which is about half of our population. The main difference between developed countries and undeveloped countries is the level of productivity of its population. In most developed countries, 80% to 90% of all able adults pay taxes yet in most undeveloped countries, as low as less than 2% of their population pay taxes. **Before you blame anyone for failure to develop your country, first ask yourself how much tax contribution you make to your country's national budget**. **Every adult Ugandan should have a tax identification number (TIN). We don't need to increase taxes, we just need to make all Ugandans productive and widen the tax base.**

At an individual or national level and from a realistic and reasonable point of view, one has to first identify their weaknesses and strengths and then use them to draw clear plans, strategies and projections on how they should exploit them to their advantage to gain successful results.

In Uganda, our strength is in our good climate, fertile soils and young, energetic population. Natural resources like oil can get used up or an alternative energy source can be discovered, but for as long as the world exists, people shall always feed and the demand for agro produce shall always be a constant factor.

Those are my reasons for investing and risking all I have on agro processing and value addition. I will leave the actual farming to other Ugandans, and limit myself to creating demand for their produce by adding value and marketing the end product domestically, regionally and internationally. It is a big idea and requires too much liability free capital investment, very low interest rates and should be very long term financing which is too hard to get in Uganda. I personally can't effectively implement it to its full potential but I have started on it with all I have got, may be the rest of my fellow Ugandans will join me along the way.

I have had this idea for quite a long period of time and I would have started its implementation about four years ago but I got engaged in the construction of a national stadium project which came with a lot of social and political complications and still has limitations in its full implementation. At times, in Uganda, people just can't let you do the right thing even if it is beneficial to the entire society. Why should a Ugandan be frustrated for trying to develop their country like construction of a national stadium? Regardless of whether one supports of the current government or the opposition, it doesn't give you a right to frustrate development of our country; rather we should join hands when it comes to developmental issues.

JUSTIFICATION FOR WRITING THIS BOOK

I am purely a businessman and I don't write books. However, in life, we do what we do mainly because of the prevailing circumstances. Many friends have approached me several times and asked me how I managed to get where I am today. That's not a question I can answer in a few statements and there was no way I could provide an explanation to whoever out there that could be asking a similar question so I decided to write this book and provide a detailed answer to that question.

Secondly, though successful, majority of the people in my country are still struggling and poor which hurts. Such a big problem needs collective effort to change the dynamics and direction of our society. It is my personal opinion that failure or success starts in the mind, thus I thought by using my experience I would write my opinion on what I think one should do to change their mindset and think progressively in life, thus the reason for writing this book.

Thirdly, I am too realistic and reasonable that I know that information is only good when put to use so I decided to share my personal opinion on what I feel might be useful to others.

NOTE: I handwrote this book in just six days without doing any research at all because it is my intention to pass on my unbiased personal opinion to the readers from a realistic and reasonable perspective on the way I see and interpret issues which has enabled me to get where I am today. Also, to give my personal opinion on what I think one should do to become successful in life.

I know most Ugandans are not good book readers but I kindly request and hope that every Ugandan finds some time to read this book. It is fully independently composed from my own personal opinion, realistic and reasonable experience. I have experience mainly locally as an ordinary Ugandan and I am aware of the the challenges we face in our day-to-day lives as Ugandans. My personal opinion on how I think we can overcome these challenges comes from my experience and knowledge I have acquired through the years.

I totally believe that the solutions to our problems should always come from us and not from outsiders. I have written this book not only from my local experience but also from my international business experience from the most developed countries like the Unites States of America and the United Kingdom. I have come to the conclusion that I should direct all my energy, channel my entire focus and share my knowledge towards the development of my country.

We all have to die one day and we are never certain on exactly when so we just have to do all we can when we are still alive so that we leave behind positive stories that will be told by generations to come. That is why I wrote this book, personally edited it to the extent of my reasoning, personally published it at my cost and I don't expect any financial gain from it. My only satisfaction will be its ability to positively change people's lives. And may be if (inn shaa Allah) with God's will, it can have great contribution to the development of individual Ugandans and my country at large.

NOTE: This is a reasonable and realistic assessment and critical analysis of things the way I see them before me from a personal opinion. They may not be facts to you. It is merely a personal opinion which may be a fact or not depending on your interpretation, how you look at things and your reasoning capacity.

2

REASON AND REALITY

GOD created man in His own image but mainly with a processing unit – **THE BRAIN** – which gives him the ability to think, analyse, judge, clarify, identify, differentiate and mainly reason in all the prevailing matters before him provided one is of full age, competent understanding and of sound mind. GOD gave us life which by definition is a challenge. In simple Economics terms there are limited resources on earth to satisfy man's unlimited wants, so, we all compete for those limited resources for survival. Life is basically a struggle and the world a battle ground for survival on an individual level, national level or worldwide. That is why we have colonialism, social, economic and political exploitation of individuals and nations.

REALITY

Reality can best be defined from my personal opinion as the facts as they are before you, looking at things as they are before you and not as you presume them to be. Presumption is a very limiting factor for one's ability to think progressively and prosper because one keeps looking for a solution to a non-existent problem rather than the actual problem at hand. One's ability to think from a realistic reasonable perspective gives them the ability to move forward in life and to survive within limited resources. Thinking realistically and reasonably gives one ability to outcompete others from the limited resources available.

One's ability to reason realistically enables them to identify the problems before them and create corresponding solutions to those problems which is the very determinant factor of failure or success.

REASON

Reasoning is for human beings, and it can best be defined from my personal opinion as the ability to think or make a natural assessment or analysis of any matter before you leading to a certain decision. God created man so perfectly that all he needs for survival is contained within him/her and it is the Human Brain that completes him and makes him superior to all other creatures. It is one's choice to use his/her brain or not.

The extent to which one uses his/her brain and thinking capacity to reason is the very determinant factor of success or failure. In simple terms, man is self-contained with all he needs to survive and prosper. One should, therefore, always apply reason in all aspects of life before him. It is so unfortunate that majority of the people choose not to apply this natural God-given gift to reason in the day-to-day aspects of their lives, whether it is challenges or circumstances of gain. It is only he that applies the power of reason that outcompetes others from the available limited resources resulting in success or failure.

Reason and reality always equal to success in all aspects of life whether it is economic, social or political aspects. In fact, the two draw the line between success and failure at an individual level or at a social collective level. Riches, wealth and wisdom are attributed to success as poverty and lack of wisdom are attributed to failure. One cannot say "that is a very poor, knowledgeable and wise old man". Rationally, that is a wrong statement or an oxymoron.

If one has lived a reasonably long life to be described as old – that is 60 years of age and above – and within that period of a fully lived life his thoughts or mind has not enabled him to positively improve his life then whatever he holds in his mind can't be called wisdom.

The starting point to the path of success is one's ability to identify his/her strengths and weaknesses from a realistic personal assessment. It is those facts that one uses to draw clear projections and goals on what one wants to achieve or gain in life.

Reason and reality are the balancing factors in all aspects of life; with proper reason that is based on reality, one can almost achieve anything in life.

3

SUCCESS

From an ordinary English definition, success is an accomplishment of an aim, purpose or an achievement. The definition of success defers from person to person based on emotions, desires, demands or one's feelings. Some will define it as one's happiness, some as self-satisfaction, others as personal fulfillment, some as being loved by people around you and others as the difference you make in other people's lives. Basically, one defines success from one's intended goal. Success can have so many different definitions depending on the reasoning of the person defining it.

I would personally define success as fulfillment of an obligation with no due regard to personal emotions.

Life is a challenge and there are life obligations which one has to fulfill with or without their emotions. Success starts from fulfillment of basic life needs like food, medication when sick and any other requirement of personal survival because *success itself is to the living not the dead and survival is the very starting factor of success.*

After personal survival, the obligation to the people in your life – that is the survival of your family and your children, depends on your ability to effectively provide for them as required or expected, which can equally be classified as an element of success. A man who effectively sustains himself and his family can be regarded as a successful person at that level. You could say man has successfully lived on earth through generations.

Generally in life, people are not desirous of bad things but rather of a good life. So, I totally disagree with success based on a bad choice; for instance, simply because one has chosen to commit suicide, that does not make it okay from a general analysis simply because he has succeed in doing so. Success based on emotions can best be defined as fulfillment of personal desire.

Success cannot be limited to personal desires because it only makes sense if its positivity or outcome is measured and appreciated by those around you. Basically, success in life is related to positivity. Society's opinion matters in all aspects of life because we live with people not alone on an island. In life, one's success is measured by others and what you say and think of yourself is merely your personal opinion of yourself to others. **Emotional personal assessed success is an opinion, not a fact.**

MONEY AND SUCCESS

From a reasonable and realistic point of view, one's success is based on one's social welfare and achievements but mainly on economic welfare in most cases. Economic welfare is directly related to the big sums of money one has.

In economics, there are limited resources to satisfy man's unlimited evolving wants. However, currently money is the number one tool of trade. As human beings, we have desires and money is like a magnet to those desires; for instance, if you want a good life, nice house, nice car, your children to go to nice schools, you simply have to **look for money.** If you earn the money, all the rest fall in place then it will no longer be a question of affordability but a question of fulfillment.

Actually, money is the determinant factor of whether one is successful or not. Those who say it is not, are either wealthy people and are simply looking for happiness from elsewhere, those born in it like queens and kings or failures that have given up on getting rich. For as long as you are alive and desire to live comfortably then you need to spend on your desires and needs for survival thus the need for money.

The size of one's pocket is the determinant factor of how well they live. This does not only apply to individuals but also to nations, that is why we have first world countries and third world countries – money is the unifying factor we all have in common today and the amount of money one has or a nation holds is the determinant factor of how much they can achieve and their level of success. Today, success has been narrowed down to economic/ financial welfare (money) of individuals or society.

In the world today, success without money is hardly called success. It may be merely an achievement either at an individual level or worldwide amongst nations; for instance when one is born, passing with good grades as a student through your education levels is an achievement, finishing school and finding a job is also a great achievement, getting married and having children is a social achievement.

However, finishing school, starting a family and being employed are not enough to equal to success. In today's world, the financial results from your education and all you do should be reflected in the size of your pocket as that is the very determinant factor of your level of success. When one has accumulated a *million dollars,* being in an international currency, he/she is referred to as a millionaire anywhere in the world. **Wealth equals success as poverty equals failure.**

4

FAILURE

I would personally define failure as lack of success or simply being unsuccessful. When you aim for something, you either achieve it or you don't; if you do, it is success and if you don't, then you have failed. Failure is non-fulfillment, defeat or collapse, which can be at an individual or national level, that is why we define a failed state as one where all the governing elements that qualify a country to be called a state have collapsed. Non-performance or simply non-fulfillment of an obligation whether it is social, economic or political is failure.

The starting point of success and failure is the mind. In one's mind, basing on the realistic prevailing facts before you, you decide what you want, what you want to be, how much you want to achieve by drawing projections on your goals, if you want to be successful or not, the level of success, if you simply want to survive or even be a failure.

At this point it is just you and your mind, not yet poor or rich. The human brain is the main processing unit with the ability to reason and critically analyse all the prevailing circumstances before us from a realistic and reasonable assessment and draw projections on what we really want to achieve and then set goals or draw a plan. **Success and failure are determined by the human brain,** depending on one's reasoning capacity. **Thinking and reasoning are the best paying jobs in the world.**

BELIEF

Belief is a key factor in success or failure. Failure due to weak belief is the worst kind because one does not give himself/herself a chance to give it a try. One is a failure by nature and choice simply because of a weak mind, a mind characterised by beliefs like it is impossible. You basically limit your mind to your reasoning capacity where anything beyond your reasoning cannot work or is impossible. You are not open to challenges or possibilities because in your mind, you have already limited yourself to failure.

Very poor minded people even rarely believe in God because they don't apply reason. The first reasonable thing in life is the universe and its creation because nothing comes into existence unless it was created thus the existence of God. People look for miracles to believe in God but the most undisputed miracle God created was man and the human brain that has enabled man go to space and develop the digital world we are living in today.

Success cannot appear from nowhere. You have to open your mind to it, believe in it, set the right projections on what you want to achieve then work your way up to achieve it. Poor people are basically weak believers; that is why in Africa, people look for witchdoctors and not jobs; majority don't even believe in success. **If one wants to be successful then they have to believe in success first.**

RESPONSIBILTY

Responsibility starts right from the obligation you owe to yourself as a human being provided one is an adult, competent understanding and of sound mind. The very primary need of your survival is your own obligation – to put food in your stomach, afford medication, housing and clothing a child/children you have given birth to.

Failures tend not to accept their responsibilities. They always shift their obligations to others such as a parent, relative, friend or even the government, and blame their failure on others. They think others are supposed to look after them and provide for them which locks their minds in a state of dependence.

This is common in African countries; for instance, in Uganda, out of a population of 42 million people, less than 1 million are paying taxes. This means that all the rest are dependants waiting on government to provide for them even the basic needs like food and medication yet they have zero contribution to the national budget despite the fact that they are sitting on good fertile soil and enjoying the good weather.

They cannot till their land for food and cash crops for income and survival and also create income for government to tax and gain ability to provide secondary collective services like roads, power, water and others.

The lack of acceptance of responsibility by the majority of Ugandans has not only led to failure of individuals but also to financial and economic failure of the entire nation.

Successful people on the other hand accept responsibility and obligation. They hold it deep at heart and in their mind hold personal obligation to change their lives by setting clear goals and projections on what they really want to achieve. They don't rest until they have achieved such goals.

Equally in line of the struggle to fulfill an obligation, one is led to the path of wealth as the end result. **One owes his country an obligation to work hard, create income and pay taxes. A tax is an obligation every citizen owes his country if indeed such a citizen wants to see their country develop.**

RISK

I would personally define risk as the ability to give, surrender or invest what you have on you with hope to gain more and this is totally based on a balance of probabilities. Failures usually are characterized by fear to take risks. They never look at what they have as capital yet money if not invested as capital doesn't hold or add value but rather is easily spent on day-to-day survival. Without taking a risk you cannot move forward.

Success and risk taking go hand in hand. Even social factors like education, working or going abroad to look for jobs all fall under the risk that one takes. It might not be in monetary form but also the decisions and steps we take in life towards success without clear knowledge on the outcome but with hope to gain can be termed as a risk.

Failures are so afraid of risking the little they have for hope of more gain. They are so scared of making losses that they tightly hold the little they have and eventually end up spending it on survival in the long run. People who work towards success on the other hand, embrace risk with hope to succeed.

If you kept $100 with a poor man, he will keep it so well that by the time you ask for it after a month, he will give you back the same $100 note. However, if you kept it with a person with an open mind and desire to succeed, he will invest that money as capital and if you ask for it after a month he will give you back the $100 but keep the profits from the gains of the investment he made with your money. In both cases what they all stood to lose was your trust if either of them couldn't give you back your money. Successful people are always willing to take a risk while failures fear risks. ***Never keep your money with the rich for free, just be sure they will re-invest it and attach a risk.***

In the world today, no one owns money. It simply rotates among us and what matters is how you look at it when it is in your possession. ***One should always look at money as capital any time he gets hold of it.***

In the circle of success and failure in the world of today, the poor in large numbers keep money in banks as savings. At individual levels, the rich borrow it in large collective amounts from banks as capital (loans) at relatively low interest rates and reinvest it thereby creating jobs for the poor. The rich use poor people's money as capital to become rich and even employ them simply because they are not afraid of taking risks. Even as investors, they use poor people's energy to multiply their wealth. ***Risk results in reward.***

CHALLENGES

I can best define a challenge as a time of difficulty or hardship towards an aim, achievements or towards fulfillment of an obligation. Failures hate challenges and are not adaptive when they are facing a challenge. In fact, they would rather not go ahead with something if they foresee a possibility of facing a challenge.

Failures are in most cases afraid of trying out new ideas for fear of facing challenges. They tightly hold on to what they have and their past. They create a routine and are so predictable in all they do.

Failures always see challenges in each and every opportunity they come across while successful people always see an opportunity in each and every challenge they face.

Failures never have the right amount of capital to invest because in their mind, if the required investment capital is a big amount, they claim it is too big to risk it, and if the required investment capital is a small amount, they will claim it is too small to make sense. The poor will always have an excuse not to invest. They always keep their money on them.

Failures and poor minded people think more than a university professor but do less than a blind man.

They tend to think a lot even when things are obvious so they always lose out on opportunities. They are never too late or too early for an opportunity but are always present and off-guard.

Successful minds, on the other hand, see an opportunity in all challenges. In fact, success cannot exist without failure; one can't claim success where no one has failed before.

Challenges to a successful mind create competition even if it is against yourself. They create the desire to even want to succeed more. A successful mind can barely rest if there is a challenge before it.

A challenge to a successful mind raises a fact of a mistake; if one is facing a challenge then definitely there is something they are not doing right which makes it a mistake. Challenges give one the ability to identify mistakes and once you do things the right way, then you are bound for success. Failures never give themselves a chance to even identify their mistakes because they always know they are right and even if they are not they never accept or own their mistakes. Thus they keep repeating the same mistakes throughout their lives hence their failure is constant.

When a successful person loses it all – may be from mistakes he/she made – they rarely stay down for long. They always find their way back up because they have travelled the journey before and know exactly what it takes to be successful. They learn from their mistakes. *Mistakes and failure to a successful mind are not a dead end; their success can be measured by how high they bounce back when they fall.*

COMPANY/FRIENDS

This refers to the people you keep close around you. In life, human beings have a weakness of assimilation because we adapt to our surroundings. One has many chances of ending up like the people he keeps close whether poor or rich, failures or successful. When we live with people, we refer to them for opinions on what is going on in our lives. One's opinion on a way forward when making choices and decisions in life may lead to their success or failure.

Poor minded people or failures have a tendency of keeping their poor, hopeless friends too close and always refer to them for opinions. It is like asking a blind man for directions. They get too comfortable with their fellow failures because they never criticise them or tell them they are failures so they all create a *failures' comfort zone.*

A failures' comfort zone is the worst thing that can ever happen to a human being because that way, you have fully submitted to failure only limited to your narrow reasoning capacity complemented by your fellow poor friends. Anything beyond your reasoning capacity cannot work and is impossible. That is why you find poor people talking about rich people, discussing the large amounts of money they own but with no desire whatsoever to ever own it. In reality one becomes comfortably a poor man or a failure.

Failures in a comfort zone become so good at doing nothing that they end up so knowledgeable in day-to-day discussions on all the unproductive things in life; for instance, they discuss the most expensive cars, richest people and countries, nice houses, fashion, sports and even about how to become rich but their discussion is only limited to the knowledge and never focus on how to improve their lives. They always have a lot of time on their hands and mainly spend it in social things like outings, functions, sports, which involve spending as opposed to earning.

Failures in a comfort zone hold a very strong bond with invisible chains that connect them together with very strong values based on pillars of weaknesses and failure as a fact they have in common. Failures or poor people are usually very good friends because there is never desire to out compete each other. They are comfortably failures in a comfort zone. They can always settle for less since they are so scared of challenges and taking risks in life. When they trust they trust wholeheartedly because they become too personal in all they do, even business.

The success minded people, on the other hand, are so determined to succeed at all costs, even if it means taking a risk with a chance of making a loss they will always proceed.

Successful people hardly trust others when it comes to investment and when they trust they don't get too personal and that limits their chances of being exploited or taken advantage of. Their decision to invest is purely based on realistic and reasonable assessment and proper calculation based on facts before them, not on emotions and personal desires.

Successful people mostly keep friends with benefits and of substance. The company they keep close is of people that add value to their lives or contribute to increase the sums of money on their bank accounts. Successful people keep company of more of business partners than friends.

Friendship bonds with successful people are usually not too strong because they always don't commit too much but leave room for doubt or fear of exploitation. Even in family, the families of poor people always bond more than those of the rich. Children of the poor acknowledge that it is the struggle of their parents that sustains them while those of the successful look at it as a mere fulfillment of an obligation from their parents and always take survival on basic needs for granted.

ATTACHMENT

Natural emotions are a weakness for failures; they get so emotionally attached to everything they do and own including people. When a poor person falls in love they love too much which leaves them with no guard at all from exploitation or being taken advantage of. This mainly comes from constant failure and being looked down on by others so the moment they get something, they hold onto it with both hands with fear of losing it. They get so emotionally attached that they end up making mistakes and in the end, they lose even the little they own.

Failures get so emotionally attached to money that they can never re-invest it as capital. Yet money in its form as paper has no value; it is the things we use it for that give it value. Money has the highest value once invested as capital but failures rarely look at it from that angle. They only look at it as a means of survival for only satisfaction of their basic needs.

Failures get so attached to property that once they have acquired it, they are so scared of losing it, so much that they even hate the thought of selling it even if you are paying them double the money they bought it. They would most likely refuse based on merely the fear of losing it without even thinking about the profit they can make from it. These are some of the factors that keep failures in a constant state of poverty.

Failures get so emotionally attached to everything that they get equally attached to failure itself. They are resentful of anything to do with success or anything that establishes the actual fact that they are poor or failures; for instance, you can call them anything but not poor, and they hate successful people passionately.

Failures hate successful people so passionately that they would do or say anything to deny another person's success. They would say the money is not theirs, they have loans, and money belongs to politicians or simply say that the successful person is on his way down. Nothing excites them more than seeing successful people collapse. They would even tell a lie simply to keep their heart at peace.

That deep rooted hatred for successful people is one of the limiting factors to move and think progressively. One focuses too much on others thus denying themselves the ability to reasonably and realistically see the challenges before them in their day-to-day lives from a reasonable and realistic perspective which may have helped them to find solutions to their problems. That is the very determinant factor between failure and success. Failures tend to focus their entire thoughts on the wrong problems.

Successful people, on the other hand, have limited attachment to things. They are emotionlessly attached – let it be to persons or material things. They are so attached to the fact of being successful and that is what drives them forward. You will find very few successful people attached to hobbies and social things. They are usually not sports fans, rarely attend social functions, and find social outings a discomfort, poor at keeping friends that don't add value, have unhappy wives/husbands, have less time for family but sufficiently provide for their families financially. Poor people have time for family but with weak financial family support.

Children of the poor people may go to bad schools, feed poorly at home, sleep poorly but always have more love for their parents compared to the love that the rich people's children have for their parents. This is because despite the fact that rich parents sufficiently provide financially, the children take all that for granted as a mere fulfillment of an obligation from their parents since they look at money and provision of basic needs from their parents as a constant factor of life. Poor people support and constantly provide for their families out of struggle based on emotions. *A poor dad has to prove his worth to his family* because whether poor or rich, *taking care of your family is an*

obligation, not an option.

Successful people are rarely attached to property. They will always sell off property as long as it makes business sense; even if one is selling their marital house, they will do so without thinking twice as long as it is a reasonable decision. Successful people make decisions based on reason while poor people make decisions based on emotions. That is why thinking is the most paying job in the world.

FOCUS AND VISION

Failures lack vision and focus. They never focus on something for long, not even their own survival. They never think before they act. They do everything on impulse. They never focus on an idea for too long for it to bear fruit. They always jump out of an idea before it can materialise. They are never patient and any small delay may push them off the right path. They desire for fast things and can always settle for less as long as it comes in fast, while on the other hand, the people who are focused on becoming successful have big dreams and a bright vision; they patiently focus on their goal until they attain it.

CONSISTENCE

Failures are so inconsistent when it comes to what they want. They never have plans and a clear projection on what they really want to achieve in life. They change their goals from time to time. This continuous inconsistence makes them lose sight of what they really want and what they need to do to prosper in life. Something as small as a bad thought about something can make them lose sight of the possibility of prosperity in what they do, while on the other hand, rich people are not only focused on what they really want but also consistent with the direction they take which influences all the positive decisions they make and that leads them to success.

PERSONALITY

Failures get too personal in everything they do. They never separate their personal interests from the businesses or work they do. They are too personal that they can forego an entire profitable business transaction merely because of personal social differences with the person they are supposed to transact with. On the other hand, successful people remain focused regardless of how personal you are or whether they like you or not. Their main goal is to exploit you provided you are the one paying, it doesn't matter what you do/what you say or where you get money from. Successful people are rarely personal because their entire focus is on how best they can exploit you.

Failures by their personality take small challenges and problems as a mountain of hardship where no problem is too small to a failure and never focus on opportunities in their lives. They direct their entire focus on simple problems

which make them so stressed most of the time thus limiting their ability to think progressively. There is life and the rest of the things we face in life; one should learn to separate the two because with or without problems life goes on. One should always keep a positive mind, and a stress-free mind to lead them to success.

In fact, successful people usually exploit poor people or failures at their very weak personal point. As you are fronting your personal emotions and passing time to make relevant decisions, the successful people use that to their advantage to move forward.

RELATIONSHIPS

Failures attach personal value to everything including people. When you ask a failure for a list of his valuable possessions in life, the first thing on his list will always be his wife yet a wife is a living independent person with an independent mind so she can even wake up one day and decide to leave you for a rich man. I find it very unfair of poor men to think they own their wives. In reality, no one can own a person, not even your children.

Failures attach too much value to their partners. I can confidently and reasonably say that this contributes to 50% of a poor man/woman's failure. Failures are so emotionally attached to one another that they lose focus on all the other aspects of life. This, at times, compromises the basic principles of survival. A poor man/woman can do almost anything to keep their partner happy which may be socially okay but from a realistic and reasonable point of view, it is very wrong.

In the world today, a woman stands a better chance of being more successful than a man; if it is a job application, most companies would hire a woman before a man. This is common in companies like banks, public service, telecommunication companies, including my company – Ham

Enterprises (U) Ltd. Women are naturally more honest, caring and patient than men, which are some of the main ingredients required for success in any business. That is why you can rarely find a man in customer care. The highest point of a woman's strength is equally her point of weakness – that's their emotions. The strongest among women is one who can control her emotions. **In my personal opinion a woman with the ability to control her emotions can achieve anything in life.**

Failure of women is to some extent a personal choice. If you are a young, cute, desirable woman, why would you settle for a failure that can barely survive on his own? Many people will claim it is **"LOVE"**.

Many people tend to define love as so beautiful and very complicated. Too complicated to understand which might be a fact to a limited emotional social extent but wrong to the level of its inconsistence when it comes to the basic realistic and reasonable principles of survival and success. You can still be a failure who is happily in love but that does not disqualify you from being a failure.

Everyone is born free with an independent brain and once we become adults, competent understanding and of are sound mind, we are free to choose partners based on their qualities which attract us to them. My personal reasonable opinion would be that in addition to all the other social qualities, economic welfare of such a person you choose should be a constant factor as a basic principle of survival.

Such a partner may not necessarily be rich yet but at least he/she must have clear indicators towards success not failure.

As a father, I treasure my daughter so much that I cannot simply offer her to a man with merely a good heart, when that's all he has got to offer her. I additionally expect such a man to sufficiently provide for her all the basic needs and a good successful future. Although at the end of the day, I would respect her independent decision to marry him if that is what makes her happy. I would not be happy about it though. We live by the decisions we make and life acts in personam, that is why regardless of how much a father loves his son, he can never serve a legal sentence for a crime he committed even if he is willing to do so. The law and system won't let him to, which is a realistic fact. A person should **never look at failure as an option.**

Failures love their partners so much because at times they are all they have, having failed in all other aspects of life. So, they hold on to their wives with both hands though the fact remains that regardless of how much you love her she still has to live and it is your obligation to provide. When she gives birth it is your obligation to provide for those children, put a roof over their head, feed them, and provide good education and all other needs to survive which totally has nothing to do with emotions or how much you love her. **With or without love, survival is a**

constant factor in life.

So in my personal opinion I strongly suggest that economic welfare should be a constant factor when choosing a partner. Your partner might not be successful yet but they must have clear indicators that they are heading there. Though in a few cases people can work together with joint efforts and become successful.

A happy heart can never be fully happy with simply emotions; one still needs to provide. Failure to provide is what breaks up most families. Emotional happiness on an empty stomach doesn't count. ***People desire to live, not survive.***

Naturally when a man becomes someone's husband and a father, he has to be prepared for the responsibilities that come with heading a family. Daughters grow up looking up to their fathers – it might not be just financial support but they feel safe around their fathers. Their fathers are a point of reference in their lives, anything that happens to her at the back in of her mind she says, "I will tell my dad". When still young, their fathers are their kings and heroes.

When they grow up and finally decide to get married, naturally their husbands are supposed to fill that post. A man is supposed to be a king, not just to his wife but to his family. Being a husband comes with a lot of responsibility as part of the package. You are supposed not only to financially provide but to also protect your wife and children. They must feel safe having you, you must be their very first shield of protection. Just like a daughter says "I will tell my dad", a wife says "I will tell my husband". If you hear your wife refer to her dad about a problem when you are around then something is definitely wrong. You are supposed to be her first point of reference. And the very first shield of most of her problems. "Most of the women want to have a king in a home, not a pawn." That is a natural fact.

Naturally a man has to work very hard towards becoming successful because being a man comes with a lot of responsibilities.

By nature society expects a lot from men – that is simply my opinion.

NOTE: God created man in a masculine way, built for hardship and challenges in life. Man has to struggle through hardship to survive; even the holy books say that man shall feed off his sweat. That's why in life people are surprised to see an old man get so emotional and shed tears. The world by nature does not expect a man to be soft but must have the ability to hold pain. They expect a man to be the first shield of protection for a woman and their first point of reference. When a man gets a problem, he is expected to work out a solution, not to cry and whine about it.

God, on the other hand, created a woman soft by nature; majority with soft tender emotional hearts, naturally patient and very caring. Women were created not only to give birth to us but to also raise us. Women create a balance in the world as men are for struggle while women are for peace. If it was not for women, this world be non-existent as men would have fought each other to the last man standing. That is why it is a natural obligation for a man to take care of his mother, wife or daughter. Though in the world of today, majority of women are more successful and more powerful than men; that does not take away the natural obligation.

Regardless of whether a woman is more successful, it does not make it her obligation to take care of a man unless if he is incapacitated.

LISTENING SKILLS AND PATIENCE

Failures are never good listeners, they never take time to comprehend, internalise, understand what anyone says or a point one is trying to put forward to them. They will always easily throw out a good business idea before they can even understand it. They are bad listeners and that is why they keep making the same mistakes over and over again.

Whereas on the other hand, the successful people are good listeners who will never let go of an idea or information. They receive good ideas and convert them into great success stories.

FORGIVING AND FORGETTING

Failures rarely forgive someone for a wrong he/she has done. You wrong them once and they hate you for life. This limits their abilities to move on from the past, misunderstandings tend to leave a very big impact on them. Inability to forgive weakens their ability to associate with others yet association is one of the main key requirements to succeed in life. When they forgive they rarely forget as they usually hold on to the past. Holding on to the past denies them ability and the strength to move forward.

Whereas successful people, on the other hand, are good at forgiving and easily let go of their past, they rarely lose out on good productive transactions based on emotions. Regardless of whether one has ever wronged them, when it comes to a good productive business that benefits them, they will proceed without any reflection on the past. **When one holds on so tightly to their past, it limits their ability to move forward and succeed in life**.

PLAN AND STRATEGY

Failures in most cases don't have a plan or strategy. They do everything one day at a time with no sense of direction. They don't identify what they want, how much they want or how they will achieve it. They are always okay with whatever comes their way so they even settle for less in most cases. They rarely think before they act because they lack clear projections on what they really want to achieve.

Whereas the successful people on the other hand, use reason and from the prevailing realistic circumstances and conditions before them draw clear plans and projections on what they really want to achieve in life. They draw a clear strategy on what they want, how much they want in what quality and quantities and what they have to do in order to achieve it.

Failures always talk a lot but lack action. They might have good ideas which they always talk about in detail but never physically implement them. When you ask a failure how to become rich, the ideas and plans he/she will tell you will always leave you in shock and wonder why a person with such ideas is still poor. *They talk too much but act less.*

That is why I said, **Failures think more than a university professor but do less than a blind man.** Some of the ideas that make successful people more successful come from failures. They always have good ideas but never have the will, means or plan to actually implement them.

5

MONEY

I can define money from my opinion as any tool or medium of trade or exchange. It can be value attached to a service offered or a medium of exchange. This can be in form of coins or bank notes. Money has become the main medium of trade and almost everything today is assessed in monetary terms. One's success is measured from the amount of money they have either in cash or assets not just at individual level but even countries are graded from the size of their budget, gross domestic products (GDP) or income per capita.

NOTE: Money is basically money the way we use it in our lives. Anyone who tries to define it otherwise using so many English words or emotions is unrealistic

and unreasonable.

A statement like **I don't need money to be happy** is wrong right from the start. To a large extent we all need money in life. You can only make such statement when you already have it or if you are born in it like kings, queens, princes or princesses. It is basically common sense that having lots of money makes you rich and not having it makes you poor.

THE RICH

From a realistic definition I personally define being rich based on income one earns and the assets he holds; where one not only has the ability to afford all their basic needs or obligations like food, medication, education plus all other needs for survival but has excessively accumulated too much money and valuable possessions or assets. A rich person owns more assets than liabilities and has more income than expenses. The rich people don't survive but live and have a reasonable guarantee of sustainability by their large incomes and assets as security.

When it gets to needs of a rich person, it is not a question of affordability but a question of desire. However, being rich can be defined from prevailing circumstances of the society where you stay, levels and classes. Qualifications to be called rich change from society to society; you can be a rich man in Africa but poor in Europe where the money that makes you rich in Africa can barely sustain you. However, when you are trading in an international currency, **a millionaire in US dollars in Africa is equally a millionaire in the United States of America**

I personally don't believe in a definition of rich from an emotional personal point of view where one says that **as long as I am happy in my life I am rich at heart.** I interpret such as merely a personal opinion of yourself, not a fact.

6

WEALTH

A rich person usually has large incomes, assets, large bank accounts with limited liabilities and more incomes than expenses but with a given level of uncertainty on sustainability of his riches. Rich people have money but when they make mistakes they risk losing it all. Rich people really put in a lot of effort to maintain their status. A person can simply be rich with a very fat bank account but with no assets. They at times hold large amount of money in paper form and spend largely on their desires though in this status they stand a high risk of losing it. The rich in most cases are after accumulating assets.

Wealth on the other hand is beyond being

rich; wealthy people have it all in terms of assets and all that rich people have but usually in very large volumes, while rich people put effort in looking for money and sustaining it. Money works for wealthy people yet on the other hand, rich people borrow money as loans and liabilities to invest at low interest rates. Wealthy people fix money as fixed deposits for the rich to borrow and give them interest. Wealthy people in most cases even own the banks. Rich people are an asset owned by the wealthy to some extent.

A rich person can simply collapse from riches to rags if they mismanage their funds but wealthy people, on the other hand, have passed the collapsing level; they stand at almost "**a no return zone**" to poverty. They can only drop to rich, not poor.

Wealth is inherited from generation to generation. The wealthy have a continuous system of income, and it is almost an automatic system that works for them whereas with the rich once they inherit and poorly mismanage money or assets, they can easily collapse to poverty.

A person moves from poor to survival, from survival to rich then finally to wealthy. Wealthy people don't have to work because in most cases their money collects them large volumes of income, because they stand on top of the money chain.

Rich people know how to make money from the system, the wealthy people own the system. It is very hard to cross from rich to wealthy. Riches are measured from the amount of money one has but wealth can be measured in time and how long one can survive without the need to work. Wealth survives through generation and wealthy people rarely collapse.

A rich person can be an employee with a very good paying job meaning he/she can be fired. Wealthy people are never employees; with wealth there is sufficiency in its sustaince. Rich people create jobs, wealthy people create systems.

I can proudly say I am a rich man today

but not yet wealthy though I work towards becoming wealthy. Wealthy people are mainly found in developed countries because a good economically sound society promotes becoming wealthy. In most African countries the rich can barely survive because of the incomplete weak economic cycles in terms of demand and supply. Social, political and long term economic stability is conducive for generations of wealth because wealth is a long term achievement.

Wealthy people rarely have huge liabilities; when they hold liabilities they are usually so minimal and insignificant to lead to their downfall. Majority of the rich people hold very huge significant liabilities and when poorly mismanaged they can drop from rich to poor.

Both the rich and the wealthy have valuable possessions or money in common; the main difference is a question of volumes, sustainability, efficiency, effectiveness of one's possessions in fulfillment of their desires. For instance, can you afford a car or a house you really desire to own or you simply settle for less because it is what you can afford at the moment due to your limited resources? A wealthy person will instantly buy any expensive thing he desires without reflecting on how costly it real is whereas a rich man will bargain and even opt to change his desire to a cheaper choice which is limited by the size of his/her pocket.

Rich people can easily drop from riches to rags due to mismanagement of resources while the wealthy in most cases can drop from wealthy to rich, but hardly drop to poor.

CROSSING FROM RICH TO WEALTHY

The rich and wealthy people as mentioned above have valuable possessions in common. A rich man has money but stands a high chance of losing it if mismanaged. They are attached to liabilities which may be bank loans, and own assets with liabilities. **When a rich person clears liabilities from his assets then he becomes a wealthy man.** He then owns assets without liabilities and holds incomes with limited expenses. This gives him a sense of sustainability from a reasonable and realistic analysis. **Money in large volumes without liabilities is wealth.**

7

GREED

Rich people rarely cross to wealth mainly because of greed. Their desire to grow so big and own everything usually costs them everything. Greed grows liabilities faster than assets. They always start with small capital investments for more gain but as they grow their riches their desire for more and more assets increases which calls for more capital investments thus more loans from the banks. Rich people see an opportunity in each and every challenge.

The rich usually drop more from riches to poverty than climb from riches to wealth. The main problem being one's inability to think reasonably but rather allow themselves to be driven by greed.

When a rich man is possessed by uncontrollable greed he ends up making wrong, unreasonable and uncalculated investment decisions which may cost him everything. From my personal real estate experience, if one has managed to own three properties with attached liabilities and has a choice to sell off one property to close their liabilities, they should sell it and use the income from the remaining two properties to move forward. But most rich people view that as a wrong decision; because of greed, they wonder why they should sell off what they already own when they can get a bank loan to buy more.

The desire to accumulate more assets faster than one's income ends up costing the rich everything.

Banks calculate interests on a daily basis, the moment the bank interest rate exceeds your actual rate of income then you are bound to drop from rich to poor.

Most rich people will admit to the fact that **maintaining riches is harder than getting rich in the first place.** It requires a lot of reasoning and involves too much risk in the decisions one has to make to maintain riches.

8

POVERTY

I would personally define poor as being a have-not where you lack sufficient resources for basic survival or being needy. Poor people can have little or nothing at all. A poor person lives below the basic standard comfortable status. Poor people in developed countries live on welfare and those in third world countries struggle to survive. Poverty can kill where one dies because of starvation or lack of medication due to insufficient funds.

If you cannot put food in your stomach when you are hungry, you cannot afford to medicate yourself when you are sick. If you cannot house yourself or if you cannot sufficiently provide for your family basic needs then without any doubt you are a poor person. **The failure to fulfil basic**

natural obligations to yourself or people you owe it to is poverty.

POVERTY AND FAILURE

Poverty is a temporary state where you simply have little or not enough yet **a permanent state of poverty is failure**. Poor people are not failures but are in a temporary state of have-not. Most people world over are poor people but not yet failures.

A poor person might simply not have got an **"opportunity"** yet. He or she may be simply looking for money in the wrong place or doing the wrong job that gives him/her poor payment which keeps him/her poor; when that changes so does his status.

A poor person might simply be looking at things before him/her in **an unrealistic and unreasonable way** so he/she may have failed to identify the actual problem before them and may have focused all their efforts to finding solutions to the wrong problem rather than the actual problem. That keeps them in a poor state but once that changes, the status changes too.

A poor person may be poor by **"default"** where one is born in a poor society, lives all their life with poor people in this poor society and gets accustomed to their ways of poverty. Basically one has never been opened to new developmental ideas that can change his/her way of thinking and focus, so they are poor by default. When this changes, they have better chances of changing their status.

A poor status may be temporary **"by birth"** where one is born in a poor family by poor parents. For as long as you are still living under your poor father's roof, you are a poor/needy person because your survival is dependent on his ability to provide. If he is poor he will not provide sufficiently and that makes you a poor person too. When you grow up into an adult and leave your father's house then the choices you make in your life can change your status.

A person can temporarily be poor by **"belonging"** where he/she belongs to a poor society with very poor conditions that cannot allow them to change their poor status, thus this will keep them in a poor state. Being a citizen of a poor country partially qualifies you as poor. Where:

> ➢ Political instability of a nation can keep its citizens in a temporary poor state where all prevailing political decisions don't favour prosperity.

> ➢ Insecurity in a society or a nation can also keep its citizens in a temporary poor state. It is common sense that one has to first be secure to think of accumulating wealth in the first place. Where there is insecurity there is poverty.

> Economic financial weakness of a nation or society where all the prevailing economic factors are too weak for one to work and fight poverty. So you are poor not by choice but because your will and drive to work and change your status is limited by the prevailing situation. Factors like weak demand and supply surely won't let you prosper.

A person is naturally attached to their place of origin. You might have money in a third world country but when you cross boarders to the developed first world countries, your money can barely sustain you so **one's poor or rich status may be defined by** *the worthiness of what he holds and from where he holds it.*

You can be poor in one society but rich in another and the reverse is the same which I refer to as a temporary state of poverty. When trading in an international common currency then it is the same status – a millionaire in US dollars is always a millionaire regardless of where he/she holds it from.

A person can easily move from poor to rich but the prevailing circumstances before him may not enable him change his status then that permanent state of poverty is what amounts to **"failure"**.

9

FAILURE OR POVERTY

FAILURE

"Failure in success" is different from **"failure in poverty";** one can fail to succeed at something or simply be a non-performer. This may be failing your school exams, failing a test, failing a job interview or failing in basic social life aspects not just limited to money acquisition and accumulation. It can be non-fulfillment, defeat, collapse or nonperformance which may be social or political. Like a fully elected poor Member of Parliament can be politically successful but economically poor.

However, failure in poverty is where one

is permanently economically poor, which can be caused by natural factors like being disabled, where one basically lacks the basic natural tools to do the needful to prosper. Disability can be physical or mental. Some physically disabled people can also be successful in life, though majority that are naturally disadvantaged by nature end up failures or poor, this maybe to a large extent but not general. **Disability is not inability.**

Poverty equaling to total failure is largely (about ninety percent) attached to the brain, one's reasoning and thinking capacity. A person might be physically sound, of full age, competent understanding and of sound mind but with total inability to think progressively. These kind of people have accepted that they are failures and look at "**becoming successful as impossible**".

They keep in the "**comfort zone of poverty.**" They are very okay with being poor and have no desire to change that. They are reluctant and negligent failures. They usually survive on as low as they can get and are not even bothered by their poor status.

They lack the desire to be rich and in most cases are failures by choice. They take life for granted in all aspects and settle for whatever comes their way regardless of how small it might be. These are the kind of people that keep families, societies and nations poor. When they are the majority in a society or country then such society or country is bound to fail. They usually don't even own their own responsibility but believe their survival depends on provision of their basic needs by others like parents, good Samaritans, government or donors, case in point is the people in most African countries.

It is okay to be poor but never okay to be a failure. A failure is not only useless to himself/herself but also useless to the society or country where they live.

Failures never have stable incomes or jobs but they would rather beg than work, they never even pay taxes. **In the world as we know it today the usefulness of a citizen** to their country is their ability to pay taxes to their governments so that they can afford to look after the less advantaged and all citizens at large, and also provide common developmental services like schools, roads and water. Failures are merely dependents on society like parasites. Failures come last in the money chain.

WEALTHY

RICH

POOR

FAILURES

Failures are the lowest of the living. They have almost zero contribution to their lives or society. It is wrong to accept to be referred to as a failure unless circumstances of your failure are beyond your control but in most cases it is not the case.

10

ROAD TO SUCCESS IN LIFE

NOTE: *At the age of 34 years now, I choose to mainly focus my personal opinion to business because I am a businessman and business is what I do and know. I am a qualified lawyer too, though realistically I am more of a businessman than a lawyer. I took gradual business steps to where I stand today. I first traded in commodities and merchandise on a small retail scale, later progressed to wholesale, moved to real estate and construction with a chain of properties both in Uganda and abroad, and finally to industrialisation mainly in agro-processing and value addition. I directly employ more than to 1,200 people so I make my opinions from a reasonable and realistic point of view basing on my personal experience.*

LIFE

Success or failure is to the living; we all live and desire to succeed in our lives as human beings. So the very first element or component of success is being alive and life itself.

One has to be naturally sound and of full age, competent understanding and of sound mind. I will divide success into two grades – primary and secondary success. I will limit primary success to success of having grown up to be a man/woman, having passed through school, having gotten married and all other social basic achievements which almost everyone has accomplished.

My entire focus and opinion is on secondary success, on a presumption that one is fully grown, finished school or didn't go to school but ready for the world and to make it big in life. At that very point when a person leaves their parents' home or care and wanders into the world to start their own life. Success defined by one's desire to improve their economic welfare (**money**), the desire to be rich or wealthy. The main question is: ***how can someone start from nothing to acquiring everything in life?***

STARTING POINT

Life is a constant factor so the very starting point is **"you"**. Before one earns anything in life all one has is himself/herself and if one desires to be successful, he/she must first acknowledge the fact that he/she has themselves. It all starts with you. Your presence and being alive is the very starting point to success, all the rest like the desire simply follow.

Your presence among the living is not enough, you must be of full age, competent understanding and of sound mind that's with a normal functioning mind.

One has to address their mind to themselves first. You draw all the focus using your reasoning ability to identify yourself from a realistic point of view. A person has to identify their personal weakness and strength before drawing projections on what they really want to achieve. If you have a disability how best can you use it to your advantage?

One has to draw a plan or projections based on what he/she has and identify weak spots in life where their personality stands an advantage. One works with what he/she has to offer.

One's nature of character – weak or strong – is the main determinant factor of what one does, not his/her desire based on emotions. One should make a choice of the business or job to do based on his/her abilities to stand a better chance of succeeding in life.

Educated and uneducated people may not start at the same level because in the world today, an education qualification is capital, so an educated person stands a higher chance to finding a job which will pay them a reasonable salary that can later be converted into business capital.

The uneducated on the other hand, can only offer physical man power as capital. They can do odd physical jobs which in most cases require more energy input but pay less, though accumulated income from odd jobs can also be converted into business capital.

Both an educated and uneducated person can raise the same amount of business capital, once they both reasonably focus their mind to it. The only difference will be that most likely the educated person has a chance to raise it faster within a limited time frame and with less effort.

A person should take time to identify their weaknesses and strengths. The faster you do that the better. You are who you are. One has to address his/her mind to that and find the best way to use that to their advantage in life. A person can live a full life and die without ever really knowing who they really were, because they spend all their lives focusing on others, and never give themselves a chance to explore and exploit their ability. That is the very starting point before even a person aims for success.

Once it comes to capital in form of money, the amount of money you have is the determinant factor of what kind of business you can invest in, not the kind of business you desire to do. If you have Shs1,000,000 as capital then you are only capable of doing a business that requires that amount of capital. If you invest that money in a business that requires more than that amount then trust me, such business will demand for more money to succeed and if you are unable to invest more money then your initial capital investment will automatically become a loss.

NOTE: Self-identification of one's abilities, weaknesses or strengths applies in all aspects of life or opportunity based on a personal realistic assessment of oneself. Otherwise one can do the wrong thing all his life. This applies to all spheres of life or failure to do so can deny one a chance to take the very first step towards success in their life.

FULL AGE

Full age means old enough and not so young that you are still in school. Old in the true secondary definition of old. Old enough to desire to be successful in life.

COMPETENT UNDERSTANDING

The natural reasoning ability of the mind. Competent enough to identify, differentiate, analyse, and access all matters before you. Competent enough to desire to succeed in life. The main component being the ability to reason in all aspects of life. Everyone is created with the brain but very few people apply reason when they are faced with a challenge. The decision to desire success is the starting point.

SOUND MIND

Meaning not mad. A person of sound mind is one that can understand what they are doing and the repercussions of their actions. Sound mind means being sane. One needs to be sane to aim for success.

GOOD HEALTH

After attaining full age, being competent understanding and of sound mind, then you must also ensure you are in good health and energetic. One needs to be sound health wise and energetic enough to chase their desire for success. Sickness can limit one's ability to attain success in life and other natural health related limiting factors like being disabled.

NOTE: One must have the desire to be successful. It should be a deep hearted desire to succeed. One must fall in love and become passionate about the desire to succeed.

BELIEVE

It is my personal opinion based on reason that belief is a key factor in whatever we do in life as human beings. The very starting point being the belief in existence of humanity and the earth we live on. Nothing comes into existence on its own; you can't believe in humanity and existence of the earth without believing in God (Allah). I am a very strong Muslim believer in God and my belief is purely based on reason. People look for miracles to believe in God but the most undisputable thing God ever created was man and the human mind. I totally believe in God's blessing as a constant factor in all we do.

One can never achieve anything unless one believes they will achieve it in the first place. One has to believe in the fact that they can be successful if they aim for it because why in the first place should you aim for success if you believe you cannot achieve it. This is one of the key factors and the most important component of success.

Failures are mainly weak believers.

CAPITAL

I would personally define capital as an amount of money you invest in a business to earn profits on returns. One starts with having a business plan, projections and strategy on the business to do, how much capital it requires and how to acquire that capital. A business should be realistic and reasonable from one's prevailing circumstances and conditions, not based on fiction and personal desire.

Capital is a key element on one's way to success in life. We always give something for something in success. When we accumulate assets and valuables then we are referred to as successful people. Capital is what we give to receive more. We invest something small and gain more with profit in return.

In monetary terms, capital is that small amount of money we invest in a business then incurs profit. A continuous systematic routine of profit is what transforms one from poor to rich. However, before we move to monetary capital the very starting capital is:

➢ yourself

➢ being of full age, competent understanding and of sound mind

➢ being in good health and energetic

Please note *"money"* is not the initial requirement for one to start on his road to success. When one has the three aspects mentioned above, **the question remains: how does one use them as capital?**

Alternative 1: A young energetic healthy person if educated can look for a formal job to get paid for a reasonable specific period of time to accumulate enough monetary capital to start their private business or investment venture.

Alternative 2: If not educated, you have to first draw a business plan and make projections and then give yourself a time frame of implementation. If in your business plan your capital requirement to start a low income business is Shs500,000 to Shs1,000,000, though young and energetic, you have no money on you and no one can possibly give you this amount of money, not even banks because you have no security, then you can do informal odd physical jobs that require man power like being a porter (helper) at a site and the like.

These jobs are usually the lowest in the labour chain and no one wants to do them but they always pay and can be a source of raising money for capital; for instance, I will give an example from where I operate business – that is downtown Kampala; businessmen load and offload containers every day in this busy part of town. For each carton loaded or offloaded, one is paid Shs1,000, though loading or offloading requires someone young and energetic. People don't want to be seen doing such odd jobs regardless of whether they are poor or not, yet it can be a very good source of capital to start a small business.

STEP A: If you apply your man power, it would take you a very short period of time to raise such money by loading and offloading cartons. In fact, it would require you loading just 500 to 1,000 cartons for you to raise Shs500,000 to Shs1,000,000.

Despite one's poor status and desire to raise capital, most Ugandans are too proud to engage in such odd jobs. They would rather live on an empty stomach for a full day than be seen doing such odd jobs.

The current nature of your status is the very determinant factor of what job you can do or can't do, not pride. You can't want to be treated and paid like a professor yet you barely completed your primary education.

Submission to the realistic prevailing circumstances and conditions before us helps us to make reasonable choices in our lives. With capital, we offer what we have, not what we don't have.

If you have managed to raise capital of Shs500,000 from an odd job, failures will look at you as the lowest of the low yet majority of them cannot even raise that much for themselves. You progress as they are laughing and making fun of you but one has to stay focused on their plan

STEP B: Then you invest the Shs500,000 in starting that small business you desire as planned. At this point you have progressed from an odd job that requires too much of your personal physical energy and man power to a small business owner which may be frying chapattis. The difference is this time you are your own boss who fully owns your business from your own personal effort and sweat. Failures, on the other hand, are always around *criticising* and discouraging those who work hard. They will watch as you start until when you succeed. Even the Holy Quran says "man shall feed off his sweat".

STEP C: Small starting businesses are in most cases small food businesses like selling fried chapattis, market jobs and the like. They usually have limited money requirement, their produce usually has high demand, characterised by very small profits and usually are not worth large volumes of money as their end products are usually fresh and perishable that demand consumption upon production.

For example, a chapatti business can barely be worth more than Shs3,000,000. I strongly advise that at this very point sell or invest your money in another bigger and better business. When you are aiming for success, you must always move and think progressively and productively. The same process shall repeat itself until when you are finally happy with your success and you can sufficiently provide for yourself and those close to you like family. Those who were laughing at you right from the start can confidently proudly call you a rich man.

If one really desires to become successful from running a business, one should really be patient with a slow gradual processes businesses take to finally produce successful results. It is always better to start small with small businesses; that way, when one passes through the gradual process which to an extent is an equivalent of an informal business educational course as experience is always the best teacher.

11

PARENTS, CHILDREN AND

SUCCESS

Giving birth to a child is the highest level of success in life. By giving birth one has produced a successor. We, human beings, only live on through our children. Giving birth creates new life and it is the most fundamental element of human survival. Becoming a father or a mother is one of the highest successful achievements one can ever achieve, all the rest are secondary.

However, it is not enough to give birth, it comes with an obligation to provide for that child all the necessary needs of survival until that child can survive on their own at a full maturity age which I might call adulthood. **Looking after your child is never optional but a natural obligation**. In most societies or countries a parent is even charged in courts of law for failure to support their children.

A parent looks after and provides for their child/children when they are still young by catering for all their basic needs including food, housing, medication, clothing, education until when they attain full age to provide for themselves and even start their own lives. Although some parents, mainly in undeveloped countries, fail at this obligation due to lack of funds to support their children or some irresponsible parents ignore their children to the extent that they do not even take them to school.

In my own personal opinion, a parent giving a child life by giving birth to that child is good enough on its own. A parent looking after you until when you attain adulthood is a supplementary effort on the parent's part which a child should be very grateful for because many unlucky children have not had that chance of their parents taking them through even nursery school.

Children that grow up in rich families with rich parents barely witness the struggle their parents pass through to provide for them. But in poor families they see the struggle and suffering of the parents especially the poor single mothers. So one should never take for granted the fact that their parents provided for them throughout school because to some African parents, this is simply a choice and they would have chosen not to provide.

Children who grow up in rich families, provision by parents is always automatic because the resources to do so are available in most cases. You will find parents pleading with such children to complete school; actually the majority of them drop out of school by choice.

Children of poor parents always have strong bonds and love for their parents because they witness their parents' struggle to provide for them. Secondly, because poor parents cannot provide a lot to their children in terms of all the basic needs, they always give their children time and listen to them. Rich people's children bond less with their parents as they take everything they provide for them for granted. Besides, rich parents are always too busy to have time for their children or listen to them.

Rich or poor, educated or not, in my opinion a person reaches full age from 20 years. At 20 years, you are old enough to face the world and it becomes your own obligation to survive. Anything your parents provide for you after 20 years, is merely an added advantage.

A man at 20 years of age, is old enough to do any physical job and earn a living with or without education. In most developed countries, at the age 18 years, one has to leave their parents' home and get an address by which he is identified. This way, one starts paying house bills and gets a sense of responsibility. It is only in Uganda and most African countries where you find 30-year-old men still staying with their parents.

When most people are asked why they are failures they claim their parents never took them to school. But in the world today, we have many rich and wealthy people that never even stepped in a classroom. So, that is no longer an excuse for your failure. You are your own responsibility; the sooner you admit that, the faster you get on your feet and fight your poor status like a real man. In fact, almost half of the top ten richest people in the world don't have degrees.

Some people claim that they are unsuccessful because they were not lucky enough for their parents to give them capital. My fellow grown-up friend, your father giving birth to you was simply enough; you should thank him every day that you are alive. You are a grown-up person who has the ability to work; put that into use and draw your map to success. No father owes a child the obligation to give them capital to start a business venture. Even if he is rich he may decide not to give you capital and you cannot blame him for that.

In fact, most people that get capital from parents always waste it thinking they can always go back for more, but the majority that start on their own and attain capital endlessly struggle to succeed because they respect such capital and are afraid of losing it so they work hard and end up becoming successful.

Success is driven by the desire to be successful. You will find that most children from rich families rarely succeed in life because they have been spoon-fed from childhood; so, they take everything for granted. Even when their parents start a business for them to run, they hardly put in effort to see such a business succeed.

Whereas on the other hand, children from poor families when given a similar chance, having grown up lacking even basic necessities, they grab such a chance with both hands and give it their all until they succeed.

The other factor that makes children from poor family backgrounds work so hard towards success is that they have lived in poverty all their lives so they understand what it means to be poor. The fear for bad or poor conditions that come with poverty makes them work so hard to attain success.

Another limiting factor for rich parents' children's success is that even when they become adults, they always think their parents shall always provide for them. That is why you find a 35-year-old man with a father that pays for his children's school fees and also provides for his son's family basic needs. Children from rich families have too much hope in their parents which hinders their ability to work hard and become successful.

Prolonged spoon-feeding of grown-up children by rich parents also retards such children. Why work for survival when your rich parents are willing to provide? This never gives such children the thought and desire to ever work hard towards success.

Majority of the children with rich parents think that their parents' properties belong to them so they don't have to work. They wrongfully think if their parents are rich they are rich too. This keeps them from working which is totally wrong thus end up becoming failures.

Children with rich parents in most cases think that automatically their parents will die before them so they will inherit their properties and assets which keeps them from not working towards success for themselves and some die poor before their parents. Some are surprised and shocked when banks claim such properties when their parents die.

It's only a rich person who knows how to manage his assets and liabilities. They always know how to balance the income and expenses, assets and liabilities. When they die, one may inherit the money, assets but with the liabilities and expenses accompanied, with no knowledge to manage them. They end up losing the properties to banks or selling them cheaply to get quick money.

One can inherit money, assets, and liabilities, but not the knowledge to manage and sustain such an economic empire. So, rich people don't just die alone but also with their property and their legacy, especially when they leave incompetent children that they did not teach how to balance assets and liabilities or incomes and expenses.

Parents give birth to us and we grow into men and women. It is never their obligation to lead you to success in life though it would be their joy to see you succeed. If some parents do give capital to their children, it is totally supplementary and we regard that as luck. It is simply an added advantage. Naturally, we all desire our parents' support which may not necessarily be money or anything physical but simply words of encouragement if that is all a parent has got to offer.

During adulthood, a person and his parents become equal, it is therefore unfair of an adult to think that another adult owes them responsibility. In fact, in adulthood your life's desires are the same as your parents'. Young children ask for ice cream while adults desire cars and houses; it is unfair for one to think another person owes him an obligation to provide things he desires himself too and sometimes a parent may not have attained them yet for themselves.

The thought that your parents owe you an obligation to make you successful in life when you are an adult, I personally do not agree with it. If they do, count yourself a lucky person. Otherwise such a thought may keep one in a permanent state of poverty thus one becoming a failure.

12

EDUCATION AND SUCCESS

I would define education as a learning system created or designed to teach one means, tools or principles necessary to successfully carry out a certain duty. Education may lead to success in life, war or to success in any anticipated challenge before you. Education can be formal or informal.

FORMAL EDUCATION: This is the kind of education we get from formally organised systems like schools, institutions, technical institutes, army training colleges and the like. These usually have Levels, Stages, Courses and Qualifications.

INFORMAL EDUCATION: The kind of education we gain from day-to-day life experiences right from when we are born until we die. As long as one lives, we are always learning. We learn right from our parents, families, relatives and from the people in the society we live in.

Informal education is so realistic that we learn from experience and experience is the best teacher whereas with formal education, most of it is in theory and mainly meant for future use or benefit.

LIMITATION OF FORMAL EDUCATION

The limitation of most formal education systems is that they really do not serve the purpose they were designed for especially when it comes to success. The major problem is that prevailing circumstances on ground keep changing from time to time so the education system either has to be regularly updated or else it the knowledge from it becomes useless to people who have acquired it because they cannot apply what they are taught to improve their lives or succeed in actual sense.

An outdated education system is useless to its students to the extent of its inconsistence with the current prevailing challenges. It is so sad that most African societies provide such outdated education and expect children from such old dated education systems to become the bright future of the nations. **It is like sending a solider to war with a gun without bullets.**

A proper formal up-to-date education system on the other hand, can be a key factor to success, not just to individuals but a bright future to a nation.

An education system should be designed purely from the prevailing realistic conditions of a society in line with the basic day-to-day society's needs. It should be a solution to the current problems of the society in line with the strength of a society; for instance, if a society survives on agriculture, then the education system should be agro based with courses on subjects like farming, agro processing, value addition and agro produce. Such an education system shall not only benefit the students but also lead to development of such a nation. A poor outdated education system does not only produce failures but also weakens a society and will never have a chance of ever developing.

13

EMPLOYMENT AND

SUCCESS

In my opinion, I define employment as any work you do or being done from which one earns an income for survival. A person can be self-employed or employed by another. For self-employment, one earns profit from the business, or income from the investment.

Employment where one works for payment for another, one is paid a salary. One can be employed as a teacher, doctor, banker, public servant, etc. Informal employment mainly in odd jobs is for uneducated people while formal employment is for the educated ones and in most cases it requires academic qualifications. Employment is mainly for the educated people as 90% of them study to get jobs for survival at the end of the day. Only 20% of the educated people create jobs or become self-employed.

Employment for a person with big dreams, bigger than being a mere employee, will always look at it as a source of capital to start his/her private business. A source that can accumulate them reasonable capital from salary income over a specified period of time through savings.

Employment is a good tool of survival but can never accommodate or be enough for big dreamers who want to achieve a lot in life. They will only be employed as a source of capital until when they raise enough capital to start their own businesses.

Employees are a key factor in the economic, social and political chain of life, whether at an individual or a society level because no man can do everything on his own. Everyone needs to employ others not only when building a business empire but also to sustain it.

Employers are always big dreamers and aim for high standards of success that make them become rich and own assets, not just income for survival, whereas employees in most cases work for survival. They will settle for as low as possible provided it is enough to sustain them.

Employers never want to let go of a good employee because it is always hard to find one and train them to what you really want out of an employee to bring you success, and growth of one's economic empire. They will always pay them not too much but simply enough for their survival and keep them working for them. Once such a good employee is paid too much they will easily raise enough capital to leave and start their own business which is never in the interest of the employer.

Employment is a very good source of initial capital for one to invest in a private business and grow to become rich or wealthy. Basically for big dreams in life, employment should be temporally, never permanent.

An employee should never become too comfortable at making others richer and growing their business empires. They should always have a plan for their own success once they raise enough capital though they should never jump out of employment quickly before raising enough capital from salary income to do their own business. If they jump out too quickly, they might have insufficient capital for their business to succeed and they may end up failures because even if they got a new job they would have worked backwards and new jobs usually come with small salaries, therefore, they may not be able to raise capital again but merely survive.

Employment salary in most cases is limited to basic survival and provision of basic needs as a salary is in most cases relatively equal to ones' basic obligations. Your social needs in most cases increase with an increment in your salary; for instance, if you are promoted to a position of a manager, you start getting a higher salary, so, your boss and society will not expect you to use public transport because they expect you to buy a car if you didn't have one and also move to a better neighborhood. One is expected to live up to the standard of their status where income is always equal to expenses. You simply live to survive and not to succeed in life.

Prevailing circumstances change; with time, one gets a family, children and that creates more needs that have to be taken care of yet in most cases one's salary never grows at the same speed as one's needs.

Employers never consider changing circumstances to raise salaries but can only raise salaries when their profits and income increase. In fact, when the economic circumstances are tough, employers tend to cut salaries. So, this limits an employee to merely survival and never to succeed in life.

A job is a mere tool of survival and never a tool of success, neither is it an asset because it is only limited to such an employee doing it at a given point in time. Your children's survival can depend on your salary for as long as you have that job but when you die, they can never inherit it or depend on it. A prolonged state of employment to an employee retards one's mind to the state of economic dependence where they are accustomed to living by salary from that job, so their bosses become their kings at some stage. Their mind becomes so locked that they cannot think of ever starting their own private business. So, they will never aim for real big time success but remain merely survivors.

Employment is a very useful tool for development of a nation and survival of an economy because employees are the driving force of the economic engine of a nation and business empires. However, when it comes to individual success, the majority are limited to mere survival and employees never become wealthy people unless if they are stealing their employers' funds.

Generally in life, we are not equal. Everyone cannot to be an employer but a rich or wealthy person can. A coin always has two sides; there has to be employers and the employees though the latter are always the majority.

What I have written is merely my own opinion from a realistic and reasonable perspective based on the way I assess things before me. My suggestions might not be facts depending on one's reasoning capacity. Every man is entitled to their opinion.

14

BUSINESS AND DEALS

A BUSINESSMAN

A businessman is a person who is in business as a means of survival in society as defined in economic terms. They invest small capital and gain returns with profits. They do ordinary trade and pass through the ordinary steps of trade as we know them. A businessman can trade in commodities, merchandise, property through real estates, forex, information and technology, among others. Business is a gradual process of achieving success. It is long term and the easiest and most common to success. One may not need education to do business.

DEALERS

From my personal opinion, dealers are people in the money system that desire fast money. There are straight (formal) and non-straight (informal) dealers. Among the straight we have brokers that include real estate dealers, insurance dealers, stock exchange dealers and the like.

Informal or non-straight dealers, on the other hand, are largely cheats and financial criminals. They live only to earn by outsmarting people with money which they call working smart. They come to a businessman/woman or rich person with what looks like a great business opportunity and before you realise it is fake, they have already taken off with your money. At times they are so good at it that you cannot even have enough evidence to take them to courts of law to file a claim.

I would not advise any young man/

woman that really desires to become truly successful in life to even ever want to become an informal dealer. Dealers always end up in prison or die mysteriously.

A DEAL

I would personally define a deal as a good, well packaged business proposal that looks so promising on the surface but when deep inside it is just a sham or a con. To me, anything in most cases that looks too good to be true is a fake deal. If, for instance, you are told that you can invest $1,000 and earn $100,000, with such a deal one will most likely lose their initial capital investment of the $1,000. Maybe if it's a lottery but even with a lottery, hundreds of thousands of people play the game but only one wins. I am a businessman who only limits his investment to businesses. I never engage in deals, not even lottery or betting in a casino.

BUSINESSMEN AND DEALERS

Success is a gradual process; you take one step at a time. It is like a child growing up; they crawl, then walk and then finally run. You cannot run before you walk; if you try you will fall. So, even with success, you need to adapt to the gradual process. That is why we businessmen say quick money does not last long and that is the difference between a dealer and businessman.

Money from deals is lost faster than it comes. It is always very exciting to get but lasts shorter than even your excitement. It is always short-term money. Business incomes accumulate gradually with a process to follow that is long-term.

A deal can only earn you money in its paper form, good enough to be spent on your desires but not to gain riches or wealth. A dealer will always live large temporarily to the extent of the mileage such earned amounts can last him.

Dealers are never rich or wealthy; they simply hold large amounts of money temporarily and usually flash it around to prove to society that they are rich and well off. Realistically, a rich person does not have to put in any effort to prove he/she is rich because that comes automatically as they progress in life. Their lifestyle improves with their progress on their way up to becoming rich or wealthy.

To a businessman, as you progress to success you leave behind trace marks on your path up. Successful people usually have successful stories to tell how they started and how they got where they are, dealers never. For dealers, it is always quick money and they rarely keep or invest it because it is always "easy come easy go". **Most dealers live large but die poor and in most cases never leave behind assets for their families to inherit.**

The worst thing money from deals does to young people is that it retards their mind.

For the young people with a lot of desires for material expensive things, quick money from deals helps them to buy things like nice cars, nice houses so fast and with no effort at all. Such young people start living large and adapt to the rich people's ways of living yet such money is not sustainable. There is always one deal at a time; if it was out smarting someone and you got money from them, they will either arrest you to recover their money or you will keep on the run for life. Trust me, it is almost impossible to outsmart a rich person twice. Rich people can make mistakes but are never stupid to make the same mistake twice.

Once a dealer is accustomed to living large like the rich do, with no idea on how to start small, he/she will sell all that is left and invest it in trying to maintain a high status because dealers usually use status to outsmart others. They always take money from people without too much effort which is a very hard thing to sustain without resources.

They will always use the rest of the

remaining money to illustrate to their peers and the public that they are still well-off. Once money gets used up with no chance of exploiting another person, they suddenly become poor.

They drop back to their original position of poverty but so desperate and dangerous having tasted a good life. They can do anything to get money. Most of them end up being hardcore criminals like highway robbers.

What happens to dealers once they finally go back to their original poor status is so sad that they lose all their friends simply because they cannot afford to spend on them anymore. Instead, these so called former friends make fun of them because they are happy that they are poor again just like them.

These fallen dealers can hardly get back up into the money chain because they lack the knowledge to the path to success like starting small. They think of and desire fast money. In fact, in most cases because of the shame, they can no longer happily survive in the same society, so they change location. Secondly, because the society they are living in is now fully aware of their fraudulent ways, they can no longer take advantage of people of that society, so, they take their scam to a naïve society but always end up in prison or die mysteriously.

If a society is mainly dominated by deals and quick money mentality, the people are bound to be failures. Every society should ensure that especially their young generation should not fall victim to this cheap unrealistic and unreasonable mentality if such a society really aims at achieving a bright developmental future generation.

15

REASON, REALITY, THE LAW AND SUCCESS

I am a prominent businessman but I have a Bachelor's degree in Law from the School of Law at Makerere University Kampala, Uganda. So, I give my legal opinion from an informed point of view. I did not cram the law like most lawyers do. I took time to understand it and always try to subject it to my reasoning capacity. I find law so interesting that I think at least everyone should have legal studies on basic legal principles. Secondly, anyone might be subjected to judgement in courts of law at a given point in their lives or we might be judged one day by courts of law. I find it unfair for one to be subjected to a judgment system they are totally blind to, so it is my personal opinion that it is everyone's responsibility to at least learn the basic legal principles.

One would wonder how the laws of a given society survive through time or what qualifies such laws to be used to subject others to judgements without rejection. What makes laws of a given society count from generation to generation? The answer is simply because they are made based on reason and reality.

Reason, Reality and Justice/the Law in all principles whether it is ordinary justice, everything is looked at from a realistic perspective then subjected to reason before passing a judgement. If you cannot be just to yourself by looking at things the way they are rather than working on presumption then you can never take the very first step towards success in your life.

From the basic legal principles of the law, 'a suspect is presumed innocent until proved guilty beyond reasonable doubt.'

'Presumption of innocence' awaits subjecting such an accusation to realistic supportive collaboration evidence and intent to prove beyond reasonable doubt that indeed one is guilty or innocent which l could call a reality test.

'Reasonable doubt', reasonable in this context is not from a legal definition but rather from an ordinary person's understanding. What is reasonable is not decided by a professional lawyer or judge but rather by any ordinary respectable member of society provided he/she is of age, competent understanding and of sound mind. If such a person is present during hearing proceedings, he must be fully convinced with no doubt that the accused is guilty or innocent without any bias whatsoever. So the law still bases its judgements on reason, an ability that almost every human being holds; that is why you find the jury in American courts are respectable ordinary members of society who are chosen to pass a verdict before the judge passes judgement.

'A burden of Proof', legally by law it is

he/she who accuses another of committing a crime that has to prove that the accused is indeed guilty by providing sufficient proof/evidence. This way, clearly the law equally subjects the accuser to a realistic and reasonable test where it is not just enough to simply make a claim or accuse another of wrong doing but you need proof to support such a claim or accusation.

Basically, the law keeps on changing or evolving from time to time due to the prevailing realistic circumstances that change as society evolves in all social, economic and political aspects from generation to generation. Historically, from the old times there was justice based on 'an Eye for an Eye', that is if you killed someone you would be killed too with no hearing procedures at all. Then came the English common law which introduced elements like evidence for proof of guilt or innocence and from this you clearly see that this was based on reason and a realistic measure to eliminate unjustified prosecutions.

NATURAL JUSTICE

The laws governing a certain society are always made in line with standard basic, social, economic and political needs in the prevailing circumstances in such a society based on reason and reality. For instance, when the white colonialists came to Africa (Uganda) they introduced the Witchcraft Act basically because it was hard to govern Africans without putting into consideration their belief in witchcraft hence the Witchcraft Act with legal proceedings, prosecutions and sentences for one found guilty of practicing witchcraft which included ex-communication. That is why when one was guilty, such a person would be chased or excommunicated from the community and left to wander out there, for example, in the case *'Slavatory Abuki V AG.'*

Based on reason, when proof of witchcraft was subjected to the law of evidence it became hard to prove or to provide evidence to support the accusation of witchcraft.

Technically, it doesn't qualify when put to the test of presumption of innocence until proved guilty beyond reasonable doubt which requires evidence. Secondly, by excommunication from society the person was denied all their other constitutional fundamental human rights like freedom from discrimination, personal liberty, respect for human dignity and protection from inhuman treatment, right to a home and property, fair hearing, freedom of movement and association and others. That is why the constitution protects itself from such laws through Article 2 which says that any law that is inconsistent and repugnant to the constitution shall be deemed null and void up to the extent of the inconsistency with such an article of the constitution, which fact takes us back to the principle of reason and reality. If something doesn't make sense then in most cases it is not right.

EQUITY

This is the arm of the Law or principle purely based on natural justice out of basic reason. From my personal opinion, l can simply say that equity basically means equality all evident from its maxims as explained below:

1. **Equality is Equity**. If a judgement is justified then that makes it just and lawful. With success, one has to be just in all aspects of their lives basing on reality to prosper in their projections or goals in life.

2. **Equity (the Law) acts in personam**. In my opinion this means that one faces his own consequences because the law doesn't shift the blame. One cannot suffer a wrong or serve a sentence for another's wrong-doing. No matter how much a mother or a father loves a child, they can never serve their child's sentence for a crime he/she

committed. The law from a reasonable basis cannot allow a father to go to prison for the son's crime even if he wished to. So does success and failure; at the end it all, it is our own success or failure.

3. **Equity will not suffer a wrong without remedy.** Basically this means that for any wrong committed, there should be punishment or for the good done, there should be a reward. In life, one should not blindly do things – whether right or wrong, without repercussions. The same applies to success or failure; you reap what you sow. Hard work can only be reflected in success and weakness can be reflected in failure.

4. **He who seeks Equity must apply Equity.** Meaning he who seeks help and protection of the law must be lawful. You cannot cheat and run to the law to protect you from those you cheated. The same applies to reason and success; he who wants others to be good to him or

be just to him must be just to them too, and that shall determine one's success or failure.

5. **He who seeks equity must come with clean hands.** Meaning if you seek protection of the law you must be legally clean thus you cannot seek help from the law if you are a criminal; for instance, you cannot commit a crime like killing and run to the law for protection. The law protects victims, not criminals. Success in real life comes to the straight business people; that is why money from fake deals and crimes never lasts through generations because it is in most cases available for a short while. If one desires reasonable long-term success, he/she should do clean businesses.

6. **Equity looks at what is done rather than what ought to be done.** The law or fair judgement looks at what is before it rather than

presumption of what should have been done. In life, one's ability to look at reality and make decisions or life projections on what they have before them and not what they presume, gives them higher chances of being successful with their plans or projections. For instance, when it comes to capital, many people want to wait for large amounts of capital because they presume to gain, they must invest a lot of money rather than starting with the little they have before them. At times, they even end up spending it in the waiting process so they end up failing.

7. **Equity looks at intent/substance rather than formation.** It wouldn't be fair by law to judge one with good intent but rather with unfortunate formation outcome. For instance, all doctors would end up in prison because so many people die under their care having subjected them to various kinds of treatment and medication. May be sometimes the actual cause of death is poor medication so everyone

would be suing doctors. The realistic fact is that the intention of doctors and hospitals is to cure people and not kill them so the law looks at the initial intent though in a few cases people file for medical negligence where it is so obvious that the doctors were the main cause of death. But it can only earn one damages, rarely sentences; and further still, the burden of proof is on you to prove beyond reasonable doubt that such medical personal intended to cause death or was negligent enough to cause death of another.

The intention to succeed drives one towards courage and determination yet with failure, it all starts with the weak mind; most poor people look at success as a miracle and in their mind, they think it is impossible to succeed.

8. **Equity imputes an intention to fulfil an obligation.** Meaning if you did something that you are legally obliged to do then it is looked at as

such. Naturally in life, we have things we are obliged to do like elements of survival; for instance you cannot be praised for eating food, looking after your children or basically expecting payment for doing the right thing or carrying out a duty you are supposed to do. The weak-minded people may end up failures because when they implement obligations, they expect payment or praise. Many children drop out of school thinking by going to school they are doing their parents a favour. It is only when they are fully grown and cannot find jobs that they regret having not gone to school. To some extent success or failure is a choice.

9. **Delay defeats equity**. Basically in judgement this is used in filing cases – whether a claim is filed too early or too late to be heard or dismissed. We have a saying that 'justice delayed is justice denied'. That is to say that if I filed a case for an order to stop one from demolishing my property or house, of what use is a judgement passed in my

favour if the house has already been demolished simply because judgement was not passed in time. So, delay defeats justice. In life, when it comes to success or failure, time becomes everything. Using reason from the realistic prevailing circumstances, one should always make the right and timely decision. This applies a lot in capital markets when making investment. *Timely and well planned investment leads to success and unreasonable delay in investment leads to failure.*

Maxims of equity are basically principles of natural justice based on reason and reality in basic day-to-day life. They came as a result of ensuring passing just and fair judgement in courts of law. They are twelve, nine of which I can basically relate with ordinary success of an individual or their failure.

The law follows reason and reality in most of its implementation so one should consider those two aspects when aiming for success in life. We have principles like that of **"Double Jeopardy"** where by law one cannot be punished twice for the same crime, meaning that if you were prosecuted for killing someone and sentenced to time of service in prison, if you come out and find that person alive and you kill him/her, you cannot be sentenced again for murder because you would have already served a sentence for that crime committed. So the law basically follows reason and ability to reason. If I am to fully relate the law to reality and reason, most probably I would have to write a full book.

These are simply my personal opinions from a realistic and reasonable point of view, which one can take as facts or leave basing on their reasoning capacity. I wrote this book in just six days simply because I wrote it as I see reality before me. However, everyone has their independent choice to take it or leave it but that remains my personal realistic opinion.

16

CONCLUSION

In conclusion, man is successfully born with nothing but life. In life, we all desire to have a good life and to become successful men and women. Unless one is born in success like kings, queens, princes and princesses, for most of us this journey comes with a lot of challenges and hardships. However, from my personal opinion which is a realistic and reasonable point of view, success starts with you as a person and requires you to have reasonable thinking capacity, a plan and strategy, personal responsibility, focus and vision, consistence and patience, good listening skills, choice of good company, ability to take risks in life, forgiving and forgetting, courage and determination in all you do, a good supportive family, a socially, politically, economically well-organised society with the right prevailing conditions to enable one succeed in life. Lastly, we need GOD'S BLESSINGS in all that we do. Success never comes cheaply even the holy Quran says, *"Man shall feed off his sweat."*

153 *Success and Failure*